T0132052

SPIRITUAL
INSPIRATIONS

— *and* —

GODLY
WISDOM

INSPIRED BY THE HOLY SPIRIT

Bernice Ware Smith

AuthorHouse™
1663 Liberty Drive
Bloomington, IN 47403
www.authorhouse.com
Phone: 1 (800) 839-8640

Because of the dynamic nature of the Internet, any web addresses or links contained in this book may have changed
since publication and may no longer be valid. The views expressed in this work are solely those of the author and do
not necessarily reflect the views of the publisher, and the publisher hereby disclaims any responsibility for them.

Any people depicted in stock imagery provided by Getty Images are models,
and such images are being used for illustrative purposes only.
Certain stock imagery © Getty Images.

This book is printed on acid-free paper.

ISBN: 978-1-7283-2435-7 (sc)
ISBN: 978-1-7283-2434-0 (e)

Library of Congress Control Number: 2019912492

Print information available on the last page.

Published by AuthorHouse 08/24/2019

authorHOUSE®

Who I am…My name is Bernice Ware Smith. I was conceived in my mother's womb by my father in 1955 and was born January 16, 1956. ---My two loving parents, Mr. West Ware, Jr and Mrs. Annie Pearl Ware took very good care of me. They are deceased now, but Oh, if they could be here now to see how I have developed and matured, they would be so pleased and happy. ---I know they are watching over me right now. And if they could speak, they would say, keep up the good work, Bernice.

---So I dedicate this book to my loving parents: Mr. and Mrs. West Ware, Sr.---I love you both. Thank you, Mom and Dad. ---To God be the glory for all that He has done.

---I want to thank God for my loving husband, Elder David Smith who has been by my side for 40 years. He is the wind beneath my wings.

---Also, I want to thank our friend Tamika Glasper for her hard work and dedication, for helping publish this book.

Love Me for Who I Am

---As I walk this beautiful earth: I think of my life and my birth.

--- Each day that God allows me to wake up: I think about the people that I must touch.

--- When I see another human being, it's just amazing of what I am seeing.

---I see them as someone that God has made: Whether black, white, bright, dark or whatever shade.

---I see them as a person with a soul full of life: And if they already know Jesus: then I can see their light.

---When I greet them I say good to see you: And I mean it from my heart, and it's so genuine and true.

--- When I see them for sure I am delighted to see them: I don't see them as dressed in silver, gold or gems.

---So when you look at me, be happy to see me: Don't look for me to be like you think I should be.

--- Love me for who I am and not for what I wear: For it's not about my clothes, nor my pretty hair.

--- Love me for being one of God's creations: Love me genuinely, with appreciation.

You Need Someone

You need someone to tell your problems to;
You need someone who understands you.
When your burdens are heavy and you're in despair;
You need someone who really cares.

That someone is Jesus, God's precious son:
He is that special someone.
He is so very, very dear:
And He's always so very near.

So just go to God in prayer;
And remember that he is always there.

When it feels like everything is falling apart;
And the cares of this world are heavy on your heart;
Just lift up your hands and begin to shout.
Lord Jesus help me, and he'll bring you out.

So whatever your problem may be this day;
Don't let the devil deceive you, go on and pray.

And if your prayers don't get answered soon;
Don't stop praying, keep on going to the upper room.
Always expect to meet Jesus up there;

Because He's that someone who really cares.
There's no one else who will really understand;
And can reach out and touch you with his healing hand.

Jesus our savior loves us so very much;
And He knows just how to give us that special touch.
God knows what's best for his children here below; So remember sometimes the answer may be no.
It could be wait, or it could be yes;
But whatever the answer is, He knows how to bless. He will never leave you, He's right by your side;
He's always near, and will forever be your guide.

A CLEAN REAL WOMAN

A CLEAN REAL WOMAN KEEPS HOUSE FOR A CLEAN REAL MAN.

First of all ladies, find out who you are in life: And then prepare yourself to be a fit wife.

--- In knowing who you are deep down within: It will truly help you as your life begin....

Take care of yourself first of all and keep clean: And please don't walk around being angry and mean.

--- Life can be hard somewhere down the road: But remember that God can lighten the load.

--- Begin to freshen up yourself from the inside out: And appreciate the joy that God has brought.

--- From now on you'll know where you really want to go: So let God take you to the overflow.

---You said that you want a real man as a soul-mate: So therefore you must be a real woman to date.

--- A real man looks for a clean real woman, my dear: And he wants her to bring him great cheer.

--- When he comes to her house, he doesn't want to see dirt and grime: He expects to see a clean house where he can dine.

--- But still a clean real man seeks to please God first: Because he knows that God will quench his thirst.

--- In life you will get the desires of your heart: But remember to let God give you a fresh start.

--- Now since you are being a clean real woman, my friend: You have won the heart of a clean real man in the end.

--- As he loves himself, he will love you: He will do all that he can to make you happy too.

--- You will always be on his mind: Because you are a part of him, you are beautiful and fine.

--- To him you are the best thing that ever walked this earth: And he sees the real value that you are worth.

--- You are worth diamonds and pearls, and all the above: And your pure heart is what he really loves.

--- A clean real woman keeps a clean house for a clean real man: And God will show the both of them, all that is in his plan.

You will have joy and laughter: And you will live happily ever after.

This Is It

This is it! Yes it is, I know!----I was in despair and didn't know which way to go.--- From the time of my conversion, I've learned God's way: But I still didn't know the correct way to pray.----- I struggled in life, while in such desperation: And I listened for God, to give me his directions.---- The bible has a model prayer from the Lord; But the enemy made it seem so difficult and hard.--- Why was it so hard to catch on? Because it's the enemy's job to make it seem wrong.--- I was blinded by intimidation and fear: But Jesus Christ said don't worry, for I am here.--- This is it, I said! Which was my inner thoughts! So just use the prayer that Jesus has taught. --- Holy is your name Oh God: I worship you, because you are Lord. --- Your kingdom come; Your will be done: This was told by Jesus Christ. your Son .--- Thank you God, for our daily bread: For everyday, we shall be fed.---Thank you for forgiving us of our sins: And we forgive others too: over and over again.--- Keep us when we are tempted and tried; And thank you, that we will stand while going through the fire.--- For the kingdom and the power, and the glory is yours forever: And then God, we will see your face in Heaven.--- God! All praise, honor and glory goes to you: For you have given us your word, which is true.

From One Birdie to Another

There once was a little birdie who was feeling kind of blue, and another birdie came by and asked, "why are you feeling blue?" And the birdie that was feeling blue said, "I don't know but what do you do when you feel blue?" And the other birdie, said, "I sing to God: songs like, "Thank You for the sunshine, thank You for the rain, thank You for deliverance from the world of sin and shame…,And then I sing "I love you, I love you, I love you, I love you Lord today, because you cared for me in such a special way, that's why I praise you, I lift you up, I magnify your name, that's why my heart is filled with praise. And before I know it I'm feeling better, so why don't you try it?" asked the other little birdie. And the birdie that was blue tried it and began to notice that singing praises did help.

So now, every day the little birdie sing praises to God.

What's Love Got to Do with It

People were made to love like God: When we love like God, it won't be so hard. Love is the greatest and that's a fact: and when you love Jesus, you can't put on an act.

So many families are falling apart: but it won't have to be that way if they have Jesus in their hearts. Well, someone asked: what's love got to do with it? I say that, the Jesus kind of love, you won't regret it. He gave his all when he died at Calgary: he died so that we can be set free.

What does love have to do with us and Jesus Christ: my family and I treat one another nice? Nice is not enough, what about when you treat them wrong: do you go on and say my love is strong? I will sing a love song to them; they will be alright: I will give them a nice dinner and gift, it will see them through the night. Treating family nice is not enough: but God-kind of love, does not treat a person rough.

What's love got to do with it, you may ask again? Love like Christ Jesus through thick and thin. Love is patient; love is kind; love is forgiving all the time. Love covers a multitude of sin: love helps us all to win.

Love Lifts Me

When I think about love, I think about Jesus; I know that his love is what freed us. He was sent by Jehovah God to die upon Calvary's cross: He died in our stead so that we don't have to be lost. Oh my God! What a beautiful love song this is! For God gave his only son Jesus so that we can live. No one else could do what God sent Jesus down to earth to do: for it took true love to bring us through. It could not have been just any ordinary man: it had to be Jesus Christ, because it was all in the plan.

People do not know how to show true love: unless they know Jesus, who was sent from above. Love is an action word, this I know: but you cannot show love if you don't know for sure how it goes.

Just the other day, I felt so all alone; but I began to think about Jesus, and the love that he has shown. I did as much as I could do to try not to be sad: but when I came to Jesus, he made me glad. His precious love lifts me so much: and I love to feel his special loving touch. His love lifts me all of the time: especially when I call him on the prayer line.

God is so marvelous and so sweet: He's the best friend that a person could ever meet. When I am sad and feeling so all alone: He's always there to make me strong. Oh, how God loves me: and in his presence I love to be. What an awesome God we serve! –He shows us a love that we really don't deserve! God loves in a way that no human can: And he's always by our side, holding our hand.

Listen

Because you are so special to me, I sent my son Jesus to die upon the cross at Calgary. I created you for a reason, and that is to obey me. And if you'll obey me today, you will be set free. Love me, hear me, and fear me, is all I want from you; and I'll make sure that all of your needs will be provided, too. My love for you is much more than any man can give; for I gave you life in your body so that you can live, live, live. Listen to me daughter: listen to me son; hold on to my hand: for you have just begun. You have a choice to live, in heaven and on earth; only if you would accept the second birth. Some people call on me for only the things that I can give them; but my desire is that they have faith and touch my son Jesus' hem. Listen! Yes! I created you! Oh yes I did; and nothing you say, do, or think can ever be hid. You can have victory through me; I'll give you power just wait-and-see.

Take heed and listen to what I have to say; I will answer your prayers if you'll only pray. When you pray, don't just call out words; but call me in faith and you will be heard. Talk to me, for I am your friend; call me anytime, over and over again. It's never too early; it's never too late; neither does it have to be any certain date. Listen to me, and I'll listen to you; for I am the only one that can see you through.

Abide In Me (God)

If you abide in me, and my word abide in you;

You shall ask what you will, and it shall be done unto you.

Hold on tight and I will take you where there is much fruit.

My will for you is much greater than you can see;

My plans for your life is that you'll help others to be free.

Love is the greatest commandment, my child;

Love everybody, and keep on giving them a smile.

Stay closely connected to me, and I will take you to Blessed places;

I will prepare a table before you, right before your enemies' faces.

I am the greatest: you know from experience;

I am the God that can give you deliverance.

So keep on holding, as you study My words;

Abide in Me, so that My voice will be heard.

A Real Good Man

In order to be a real good man: you must live according to God's command. Yes, Adam fell in the Garden of Eden for sure: but you can be strong and explore. A real good man should seek to please God, our Father: he should not be misled by a sister or a brother. He should pattern his life after what God has to say: and when he does so, then he won't be led astray. A real good man should love God first: and for the Word of God, he will hunger and thirst. ***After a real good man finally finds himself: then he won't desire if the world says go left. Keep your eyes on doing the right thing in life: and you won't be so easy to be enticed. A real good man should know how to pray and be a winner indeed: because the enemy want to see you lay down and never succeed. You should have big goals and dreams: and believe God to help you to choose your queen. When you find that wife, treat her as your own flesh: and when you do this, you truly will be blessed. Remember when you are united as husband and wife: you are joined together, not just for you but for Christ. Make sure that you're on one accord: and that you both accepted Jesus Christ as Lord. You might ask, what does that have to do with my purpose and plans? I know what I want, it's in my hands. I must say that life is not all about you: but it is about God and what He has for you to do. So come to realize and get on board good man: And let God show you, and lead you to the Promised Land.

A Real Good Woman

From the beginning of God's creation: the woman was perfectly made; and this is the revelation. For she was a real good woman, being part of God's plan: she was created from the rib of Adam, the man. Yes, she fell in the Garden of Eden too; and God allowed her to really go through. Now she can find out that there is more: and after doing so, then she can begin to explore. After finding out who she really is; then God will bring her to the right man to marry and live. A real good woman was created by God, and she can be trusted because Jesus is her Lord. As she goes from day today: she will have a desire in her heart to seriously pray. She's a virtuous women who has Jesus in her heart: and now she can be trusted, as the plan was from the start. The real good woman, you can always trust: and for no other man will she ever lust. God's will shall always be on her mind: and she will be genuine, loving and kind. She will love her husband always and obey him: he will always love her because she is truly a gem. This special woman indeed is truly unique: and when the man finds her, she's found for keeps. A real good woman is to be praised: because she is fearfully and wonderfully made.

Break Every Chain

As I go from day to day: I asked the Lord when I pray; give me the strength to run this race: because there are obstacles that I have to face. The enemy sends this and that to distract: chains of bondage trying to hold me back. But God, with His dynamic power: tells me to just pray each day, at least for an hour. So I fight the enemy with conquering prayer. Knowing that the enemy will try to hit me anywhere. I call on the name of Jesus with force: for the enemy tremble at that name of course. I say, break every chain! Break every chain! He loses his grip and strength I regain. Resist the devil and he will flee from you: Use your power, and see what Jesus will do. I am blessed to be in the army of the Lord: and knowing Him helps me to stay on guard. With Jesus as my Savior and the Holy Spirit as my friend: this fight I will continue to win. The chains have been broken and I am set free: strong in the Lord I will always be.

If I Had Wings of a Dove

God, you are the one and only God.

There is no one else to be called Savior and Lord. As I walked down the road of despair: God, my Savior was the one that truly cared. -I could hardly see my way: neither could I even pray. The path was so dark and gloomy too: So much fear until I didn't know what to do. So I on that day I said to God up above: just give me the wings of a dove. -I wanted to fly away from all of that fear: but God didn't let me, he said standstill I'm here. I said, oh my Lord, this test is so hard: but God said after this you will have a new start. In an encounter with the enemy, I was shook and shaped. And through it all I've got the victory. From now on I watch what comes my way: And right away, I began to pray. Oh now, if I wished that I had the wings of dove: I can just pray and stay hidden in God's love. Wings of a dove cannot keep you from harm: But just run to God and stay wrapped up in his arms. Whenever you're faced with hard struggles in life: Just trust in God and His son, Jesus Christ.

Turn Your Pressure Into Power

In this life you will have some ups and downs: also you may have to wear a frown. It may get so hard at times too: but never give up; keep on pressing, for Jesus will see you through. The pressure may get too hard to bear; but as long as you have Jesus, you'll know that he cares. It says in the Bible, for us to trust in his word. He cares and his voice must be heard. Take a day at a time in your life with Jesus Christ: never turn a loose His hand because His way is so nice. ---Turn your pressure into power today: get on the job and press and pray. Why did I say job, my friend? Because praying is how the Christians win. ---The pressure was sent for you to get great power. ---So pray, sing, and praise, so that the blessings will be showered. --Showered down from heaven, from God our master: and when you obey God; the blessings will come faster. The enemies thought that they had you until you pressed and prayed. They became confounded when you went in prayer before God and laid.---Turn your pressure into power, my dear: press and pray for our God to hear. Sometimes we cry because we are so overwhelmed; but please let every tear be shed to the Great I am. ---God always hears the cry of his child: He doesn't want you to be said: but wear a smile. When you know that you are not alone: you will talk to Jesus like talking to your best friend on the phone. No one wants pressure at all: but it will help you, although you may fall; but by falling you can't help but to go on your knees; and when you do so, God will be pleased.

I Run to the Water (The Well of Living Water)

Earnestly God I seek your face. I run to the Waters: my healing place. My soul hungers for you in a dry and thirsty land: I know that you haven't left me; you're still holding my hand. Here is my cup to draw from the living waters. Please hear my cry, for I am your daughter. As I come to you with a heart of desperation, please give me what I need to resist temptation. When I try to do good: evil is always there; but I thank God for He truly cares. Running to the water brings me such peace. And I know that when I get there, that there will be a feast. It's amazing that you can drink from the Master's spring: and if you'll notice, He will give you songs to sing. I am happy to have Jesus Christ in my heart: For I will always seek Him and never depart.

Wake Jesus Up in You

Examine yourself and if you seem to have a problem within yourself to where it is hard to get in God's presence. It seems like even your prayers are not going any further than the ceiling. Well that is when you will seriously have to steal away. Find a place alone with God. God is our source. He is where we get our inner most strength from. He is our all in all. And that is when you will need to fast and pray. The best kind of fast for me, I've noticed is no food: just water. Run to the water and the father will hear your cry and give you peace. Peace like a river. Now, wake up Jesus within you. You let him go to sleep, you have to wake him up. You may feel like he has left you, but no! He will never leave you nor forsake you. You know, God smiles when we praise, worship, and become intimate with him.

SuperBowl

Sunday mornings! Oh what joy! I wake up with excitement and rejoice. Just God, Jesus, and the Holy Ghost is all that I need: they always help me to succeed. Power! Power! Power! From heaven above: and the Trinity brings healing and love. For God so loved the world that He gave his only son: for I am so glad that I am a chosen one. Jesus dies for each and every one of us: This is why, in Him we all must trust.

Well, why do I say Super Bowl today? Because it's a supernatural act of God that is teaching me by his grace. Favor! Favor! Is on my life my friend: and I thank God, for I've been born again. Well, what is it about Super Bowl that I am trying to say? The supernatural act of God is teaching me how to pray. A bowl is made to hold an object or solution: it reminds me of God's great hands holding me and his great resolutions. I am whole and I am free: And being a child of God, I have the victory. Super! Super! Supernatural is here! God's supernatural is not to be feared.

One Day at A Time

One day at a time is yours for free: One day at a time, God will keep thee. As you wake up each morning, don't forget to pray: Just began to thank God for letting you see a new day. His amazing grace is there to protect you: So always remember that he will see you through. Never let the cares of this world get you down: because there is no need to wear a frown. And smile for it's a gift that comes from above: it's shows other people that you have God's love. Smiling is a gift that expresses the wonderful secrets of the heart: if you give a smile away, they will never depart. A smile from you makes another person smile too. A beautiful

smile will help you through the day: and truly it'll help you along the way.

It's Like Heaven on Earth

After accepting Jesus Christ into your life: You should allow yourself to be like Him by walking in the light.-There's the sun, the moon, and stars shining from the sky up above: And as they shine we can feel God's love.—And that is how heaven is to me:-Heaven is like just being free: Free to love, laugh, and live: Free to share with others and give: Heaven is like being quick to forgive others: Forgiving all of your sisters and brothers. What a wonderful God we serve: One that we pray to and our prayers are heard.-I dance, sing, and praise our Lord: and He gives me joy down in my heart. --Heaven is like being with our loved ones: Just enjoying life and having fun. When I think of heaven and how I desire for things to be: I know that it's all inside of me. God, Jesus, and the Holy Spirit is my guide: And they are the reason why I am still alive. God sent angels that I never met before: To come and knock at my door. -Some even knocked with a prayer to pray: They had such a beautiful smile upon the face. You too will be shown the Master's glory: As you stay close to Him, He will give you a story. -I wouldn't take anything else for the experiences that I've had: For my Lord and Savior, Jesus Christ has made me glad.

No Room for Isolation

For years I notice myself in isolation, and I even questioned myself on why is this so hard to change. Since I've accepted Christ into my life, I have a listening ear to hear God's voice. He speaks to me and gives me life changing ideas and strategies. Ideas that are so wisely put together. There's no way that I could think of such things on my own, but God!

You see, God chooses people to do a special work for Him according to the abilities and gifts that He has placed inside of them. The God-given gifts even bring joy to your own heart and you are the vessel that's being used. Your gifts make room for you.

Printed in the United States
By Bookmasters